The NOAH'S ARK A.B.C.

and 8 Other Victorian Alphabet Books in Color

Edited by

Ruari McLean

Dover Publications, Inc., New York

Introduction

The theme of this book is drawings containing or combined with the letters of the alphabet. The letters of our alphabet—or, rather, alphabets, since we use several different ones together (capitals and lower-case in roman and italic) on any printed page—are themselves drawings, which once represented objects like hands and houses, but have gradually evolved into shapes in their own right. The main interest of the illustrations in this book, however, is not in the way the letters have been drawn, but in the pictorial backgrounds. The letters themselves are mostly sturdy and self-supporting; they are there as plain statements, factual rather than imaginative. The information and amusement lie in the surrounding pictures. In this selection, only the artist of *The Globe Alphabet* (we do not know his name) and Walter Crane (who drew two of the alphabets in the book) have tried to design their pages as a whole. The globe alphabet is particularly successful, and the bold red letters make a splendid contribution to the pages. Crane's use of the letters, on the other hand, is surprisingly feeble, and the letters themselves are not at all well drawn.

The alphabets chosen for this book were all first published between about 1865 and about 1877. They were published as "toy books," a special kind of picture book for children which was developed in the 1860's and followed a fairly standard pattern of make-up: the page size was almost square, about 10½ inches deep by 9 inches wide, and the books consisted of six or eight pages of pictures in full color, with accompanying pages of plain text, never illustrated. They were bound in brightly colored paper covers, usually with the title in large-size decorated letters, like fairground lettering. Purely pictorial covers, which one might have expected, were rarely used. The books were sold originally at 6d, or 1s mounted on linen ("indestructible"), but they soon went up to 1s and 2s, respectively.

These were essentially picture books, not reading books. They were also conceived and designed purely as children's picture books; so many books for children up to that time still looked like books designed for adults. They also represented a step forward in the history of children's book publishing because at last the publishers concerned (first George Routledge and Frederick Warne, then soon afterward all the other children's book publishers) began to exploit the possibilities of color printing to produce superb plates cheaply for children. Color printing had become a commercial reality in the early 1840's, but no one had yet exploited it for a mass market—which itself was a new phenomenon. It required publishing courage, because very large quantities had to be printed in order to keep the unit cost low. George Routledge is said to have told Walter Crane that he made no profit on toy books, and could not do so unless he sold at least 50,000 copies. This sounds like a publisher's ploy, trying to sound pathetic and get the artist to accept a

Published in Canada by General Publishing Company, Ltd., 30 Lesmill Road, Don Mills, Toronto, Ontario. Published in the United Kingdom by Constable and Company, Ltd., 10 Orange Street, London WC 2.

The Noah's Ark A.B.C. and 8 Other Victorian Alphabet Books in Color is a new work, first published by Dover Publications, Inc.,

in 1976. The original publishers and dates of the nine alphabet books are given in the Introduction (above).

International Standard Book Number: 0-486-23355-3
Library of Congress Catalog Card Number: 76-9221

Manufactured in the United States of America
Dover Publications, Inc.
180 Varick Street
New York, N. Y. 10014

lower fee; however, some of Routledge's account books survive[1] and show that, for example, the first edition of the *Alphabet of Trades*, in 1865, was 10,000 copies; the second edition, in 1868, consisted of 5000 copies; and a third edition, in 1872, was 9950 copies. The first edition of Crane's *Noah's Ark A.B.C.*, in 1872, was also 10,000, with a second edition in the same year of 5000, and by 1876 three further editions of 5000, 4000 and 4000. First editions were rarely as much as 10,000 copies, and hardly ever more, until the picture books of Randolph Caldecott and Kate Greenaway, with printing help by Edmund Evans, became runaway best-sellers some years later.

Picture books were often commissioned, and the publishing risk carried, by the big wood-engraving and printing firms like the Dalziels, Leighton Brothers and Edmund Evans. The latter relates in his *Reminiscences* that Caldecott's first two toy books, which Evans produced in 1878, were printed in editions of 10,000 copies each, but were sold out before he could get another edition printed. Caldecott's toy books became so popular that Evans was soon printing first editions of 100,000 copies, and I think it is true to say that the Caldecott toy books have remained in print ever since. Edmund Evans also recounts that when he decided to print 20,000 copies of the first edition of Kate Greenaway's *Under the Window* (not a toy book, but a bound book priced at six shillings) he was laughed at by George Routledge, to whom he had entrusted publication; nevertheless, they soon found that he had not printed nearly enough copies to satisfy the first demand, and for a long time Evans could not print copies fast enough to keep up with the sales.

Apart from the two alphabets by Walter Crane (who was only 27 when the *Noah's Ark A.B.C.* was published), the drawings in this book were not signed, and in most cases we do not know for certain who the artists were. The drawings are charming and full of information about the mid-Victorian times in which they were drawn and which they illustrate. They have qualities of simplicity and directness which contrast pleasingly with Crane's far more skillful, yet also more self-conscious, style of drawing.

The *Alphabet of Trades*, engraved and printed from wood by the Leighton Brothers, was No. 2 in the Routledge Shilling Toy Book series and, according to the Routledge accounts, was first published in 1865, in an edition of 10,000 copies.[2] It is surprising to find that a modern parallel, mostly with the same skills, exists for nearly every trade shown. Even an "organman," and certainly similar kinds of itinerant street musicians, can still be found among the "buskers" on London streets. Brewers' draymen still lower barrels of beer into cellars using the same gear as in X. But how many modern children have seen a hatter at work, or a lamplighter, or a milkmaid carrying pails of milk on a yoke, or a professional shrimper with a basket on his back, or a yeoman (i.e., a farmer) riding round his fields on a horse? The drawings of the blacksmith and the knife-grinder, with their equipment and tools, are particularly well done.

The Railway A B C was published as No. 1 in Warne's Aunt Louisa's London Toy Book series, at a shilling, printed in colors by Kronheim; the British Museum copy was received in January 1866, so it was probably published for Christmas 1865.[3] Railway alphabets were very popular at this time: almost the first toy book ever drawn by Walter Crane was *The Railroad Alphabet* in 1865, when he was only 20. The drawings in the alphabet reproduced here give us a good idea of some of the differences between railway travel then and now, but unfortunately the artist cannot be entirely trusted for his detail. For example, the row of taps on the smokebox door of the engine in E is mythical. This sort of engine was designed about 1846. The open cab in E and F is correct: the enginemen did not like being enclosed, and open cabs persisted until the turn of the century. Charing Cross Station (which has now, I believe, the highest number of trains going in and out of it at rush hours of any station in the world), shown in P, is still recognizable; it had been built in 1863 by John Hawkshaw, the engineer who also built Cannon Street Station. In the alphabet toy books, Q nearly always stood for Queen, and they can often be dated approximately by her appearance: as Queen Victoria grew older, so the drawings had to be gradually changed in subsequent editions. One wonders, looking at C ("Where William

---

[1]Now housed in the D. M. S. Watson Library, University College, London. I am most grateful to Dr. R. J. Faith for her help and skill in extracting facts from these documents for me.

[2]It is reproduced here from *Routledge's Picture Gift-Book, containing Alphabet of Trades, The Three Little Kittens, Nursery Songs, and The Five Little Pigs,* London, George Routledge and Sons, n.d.

[3]*The Railway A B C* and *The Globe Alphabet* are reproduced here from *Aunt Louisa's London Picture Book. Comprising The Globe Alphabet. Nursery Rhymes. The Railway A B C. Childhood's Happy Hours,* London, Frederick Warne and Co., n.d.

must stand/With your coat on his arm and your bag in his hand"), how many of the young readers of *The Railway A B C* had a William to carry their bags? And finally, it is to be noted that in this alphabet, author and artist were defeated by Z, and omitted it.

The *Alphabet of Flowers* was No. 15 in Routledge's Shilling Toy Books, and was engraved and printed from wood by Leighton Brothers. It was probably first published about 1868. It is charming, but it is another example of the common inability of Victorian illustrators to draw children truthfully. The heads, apart from having standardized and idealized features, are often far too big, as if they had been drawn from above. The flowers in this book are far better drawn than the children; it is full of delightful evocations of Victorian gardens—mostly, but not entirely, of a superior kind, well stocked with statues, urns, rustic seats, peacocks, gardeners and fairies.

The *Farmyard Alphabet,* also engraved and printed from wood by Leighton Brothers, was published by Frederick Warne, probably about 1869. This was another highly popular subject for pictorial alphabets, and many variations appeared in every series. The countryside was then for the first time being opened up by the railways, and was represented in idealized form for town-dwellers in innumerable picture books, especially those illustrated by Birket Foster. The drawings in this alphabet are much better than in most of the other anonymous ones and may have been by Harrison Weir, whose specialty was animals. As always, the letter Z—quite apart from X and Y—was a ticklish problem, and the solutions in this and in *John Bull's Farm Alphabet* indicated the desperate straits to which the "poet" was reduced.

John Bull's Farm Alphabet was No. 52 in Aunt Louisa's London Toy Book series, published by Warne, and the British Museum copy was received on 15 February 1876. It was printed by Kronheim, and the artist was L. C. Henley, whose name I have not come across elsewhere: he may have been one of Kronheim's staff artists. There is much more information about farm life in these drawings than in the *Farmyard Alphabet,* and in Q there is even a child that looks like a child. There is a mass of well-observed detail throughout: e.g., the abandoned rimless wheel in B, the Silky Bantam in F, the pole under the haycart to stop it running backwards, in W, and the "zmall things" in Y and Z. The background scenery in A looks very like a corner of the Sussex downs, where

perhaps the whole book was observed, despite the Yorkshiremen dragged (quite incorrectly) into Z. "Zmall" for "small" could be expected from a Somerset countryman, but that would not scan so well.

Walter Crane's Absurd A.B.C. was engraved and printed from wood by Edmund Evans, by far the most sensitive and intelligent of the London engraver-publishers, and published by Routledge in 1874. All Crane's toy books were drawn for and printed by Evans, who wrote of Crane in his *Reminiscences:* "He had only just left J. W. Linton's establishment for engravers . . . I availed myself of Walter Crane's talent at once: he did all sorts of things for me—he was a genius. The only subjects I found he could not draw were figure subjects of everyday life." This may have been true at first, but some of Crane's later drawings in toy books of everyday life in Victorian London look splendid to our eyes. No doubt they then seemed overshadowed by the sumptuous richness of his illustrations of fairy-tale characters. In the *Absurd A.B.C.* (Routledge's accounts show that the first edition was 20,000 copies; there is no reference to subsequent editions) Crane has found a most ingenious way to organize his designs, and has even made an attempt, on some pages only, to integrate the letter with the drawings. He let himself go in the drawing to an unusual degree; the drunken grenadier at the inn, the old person that cobwebs did spy, and Tom, the son of the piper, are delightful comic creations. The illustrations were printed by Evans in four colors only—gold (chiefly for the letters), black, red and yellow. Blue is nowhere used on the inside pages, but it was used on the cover, where gold was not used. One wonders why black was used as a background, since it seems to need all Crane's gaiety and skill in filling the space not to be overpowered by it. However, he does succeed, if only just, and every page is worth examining in the closest detail.

Walter Crane's Noah's Ark A.B.C., also engraved and printed by Evans, was published by Routledge in 1872. It is simpler in style than much of Crane's work and looks earlier than its published date; it may have been based on earlier drawings. The ornate beak of the ark, shown in the first picture, and the glimpses we get of it on three other pages, are characteristic of Crane's decorative imagination.

The Globe Alphabet was printed (in England) in chromolithography by Emrik and Binger. It was No. 56 in Aunt Louisa's London Toy Books, published by

Warne in 1876.[4] It is the most decoratively designed of all the alphabets, with a wider range both of colors and of geography. Curiously, it is the third of these books to include an organ-grinder, who is here under I for Italian, but is Swiss (under Heather!) in the *Alphabet of Flowers*, and under O in the *Alphabet of Trades*. The drawings of the shop in I J, the mill and the organ all suggest that the artist was not English; he may have been German, and the book may also have been issued in Germany. Many toy books were also translated into French, and nearly all appeared in the United States, not always with the permission of the original publisher. One of the most valuable pictures in this book is the xylographer, since contemporary pictures of wood engravers are rare, particularly in color. A xylographer is also depicted in color in William Nicholson's pictorial *Alphabet,* but it does not show his gear as well as this picture does. The globe between the lamp and the woodblock—the block sits on a leather pad for ease of turning and steadiness—was filled with water to throw a concentration of light on the part being engraved.

Aunt Louisa's Alphabet was printed by Kronheim for Warne, and was published late in the Aunt Louisa series, probably about 1877. In some ways it is the most exciting, visually, of the whole lot. Because it is so factual, it escaped the sentimentality that is an off-putting factor in so much work of the late nineteenth century. *Aunt Louisa's Alphabet* is effectively an illustrated guide to the junk shops of today: it would be an interesting competition to see how quickly a complete collection of all the items illustrated could be put together, and at what cost. The items to hang on the Christmas tree would probably be the most desirable—and the most difficult to find.

And so, back to Zachary in the *Farmyard Alphabet,* shutting the gate: "Good Night, little children; it's getting quite late."

[4]See Footnote 3.

RUARI MCLEAN

For help and information generously provided while I was compiling this book, I am grateful to Dr. R. J. Faith, and to Miss Joyce Irene Whalley of the Victoria & Albert Museum Library. The following recently published books also provided useful information and enjoyment:

Massin, *Letter and Image,* London, Studio Vista, 1970.

Ruth M. Baldwin, *One Hundred Nineteenth-Century Rhyming Alphabets in English,* Carbondale, Southern Illinois University Press, 1972.

Joyce Irene Whalley, *Cobwebs to Catch Flies,* London, Elek, 1974.

Isobel Spencer, *Walter Crane,* London, Studio Vista, 1975.

CONTENTS

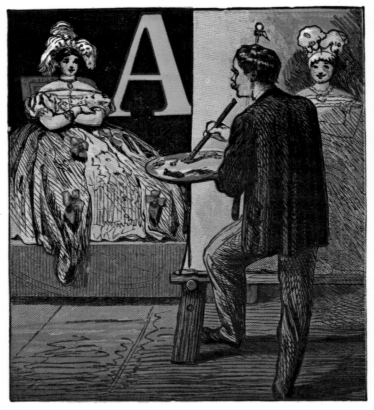

A is an Artist, who copies so well,
That likeness from sitter one scarcely can tell.

B is a Blacksmith, who hammers away,
With a clang and a clatter, throughout the whole day.

C is a Cobbler, who sticks to his last;
His work strong and neat, though he stitches so fast.

D is a Dressmaker, whose work seems but play,
For she's making a dress for her own wedding day.

ALPHABET OF TRADES

E, an Engineer, files and hammers away,
Moulding iron and brass as though they were clay.

F is a Flower-girl, fair and modest as well,
Who with a sweet voice cries "Flowers to sell."

G is a Gardener of such skill and care,
That no flowers or plants with his can compare.

H is a Hatter, who alters the brims
And crowns of his hats, to suit fashion's whims.

I is an Innkeeper, with flagon of ale,
Which J, the Joiner, will drink without fail.

K, a Knife-grinder, sharpens all kinds of blades,
Razors, scissors, and tools for all sorts of trades.

L, a Lamplighter, nimbly skips up and down,
And lights in a twinkling the lamps of the town.

M is a Milkmaid, whose heart is as light
As her milk is pure and her cans are bright.

N is a Newsboy, who plies well his calling,
And "Latest Edition" always is bawling.

O, an Organ-man, plays tunes grave and gay,
Content for his pains with very small pay.

P is a Postman, whose rat-tat so smart
Causes sorrow and joy in many a heart.

Q, a Quarryman, splits up a mass
Of marble or granite as though it were glass.

R is a Reaper, before whose keen blade
Falls the ripe corn God's goodness has made.

S is a Shrimper, who gleans from the sea
The shrimps and the prawns that give zest to our tea.

T is a Tinker, who, when holes are found
In old pots or kettles, will soon make them sound.

V is a Verger, courteous and grave,
Who points out the tombs of the pious and brave.

W, a Washerwoman, always is seen
At her tub, hard at work, rubbing dirty things clean.

X stands for excellent, when on barrels of beer;
So the more x's, the better the cheer.

Y is a Yeoman, whose fields are well till'd,
His men are well housed, and his barns are well fill'd.

Z stands for Zoologist, also for Zany;
So please take your choice: that's if you have any.

A is the Arch; underneath are the rails,
To carry the passengers, baggage, and mails.

B is the Bell, which rings loudly and clear,
And tells that the train which we wait for is near.

C is the Carriage, where William must stand
With your coat on his arm and your bag in his hand.

D is the Driver, just starting the train,
He cares not for cold, nor for wind, nor for rain.

E is the Engine, that wondrous machine,
So prettily painted with scarlet and green.

F is the Fire; just look at the stoker,
He is stirring the coals with a long iron poker.

G is the Guard, all in silver and blue,
Telling his mate that the next train is due.

H is the Horse-box, a neat little room,
Where the pony may travel with Harry his groom.

I is the Iron of which rails are made,
And J is the Junction where two lines are laid.

K is the Key, which fastens the door
When the carriage is full, and will not hold one more.

L is the Lamp, which the porter will light
If we pass through a tunnel or travel at night.

M are the Mails from all parts of the land,
To the General Post in St. Martin's-le-Grand.

N is the News-boy, who cries "Here you are!
Punch, Times, Daily Telegraph, Standard, and Star."

O are Officials, in uniform coats,
With pencils, and paper on which they take notes.

P is the Platform at Charing Cross station,
Which has gained for the Builder a great reputation.

Q is the Queen, just come out of the train,
And her carriage will take her to Windsor again.

R are the Rails which the workmen are laying;
They labour all day, and have no time for playing.

S is the Steam which comes out of the funnel,
And gets into our eyes when we go through a tunnel.

T is the Tunnel which runs through the hill,
And is hollowed and built with most wonderful skill.

U is the Uproar the boys like to make,
When they hear the trains rattle, and see the arch shake.

V is the Viaduct, built with great pains,
To carry the Railway which carries the trains.

W is the Watchman, with flags in his hand,
Who ten times a day at the crossing must stand.

X is the Excursion from Brighton which comes,
With passengers, soldiers, and rifles, and drums.

Y is the Yeoman, just come up from Kent,
He farms his own land, and he never pays rent.

A for Anemones, telling of Spring,
And the gladness and brightness that gay colours bring.

B is the Blue-bell, that sparkles with dew,
And carpets the ground with its flowers of blue.

C for Convolvulus, children's delight,
Which opens in daytime, and shuts up at night.

D is the Daisy that grows in the lanes,
Of which Jessie and Sarah make rosy-tipp'd chains.

ALPHABET OF FLOWERS

E is the Eglantine briar, so sweet,
Which Emily trains o'er the latticework neat.

F is the Fox-glove, which Tom stays to pop,
Though his mother has sent him for bread to the shop.

G is the Grass which the sheep love to eat,
And which makes for young Robert so pleasant a seat.

H is the Heather, red, purple, and grey,
Which reminds the poor Swiss of his home far away.

I is the Ivy that gives the cool shade,
Where John eats the soup that his daughter has made.
J is the Jonquil, that grows by the brook,
At which Ellen and Caroline longingly look.

K is the King-cup, as yellow as gold,
Which Katherine prizes as treasure untold.

L is the Lily, with leaves of bright green,
Which we'll wreathe round the head of our sweet
Birthday Queen.

M is for Mignonette, sweet-scented weed,
Which Mary has raised in her garden from seed.

LEIGHTON, BROTHERS.

N for Nemophila, lovely of hue,
Like the sweet summer sky in its delicate blue.

O Oleander, the Gardener's pride;
He thinks it the finest in all England wide.

P is the Primrose which comes in the Spring,
When blackbirds, and thrushes, and goldfinches sing.

Q for Quince-blossom which naughty young Ned
Pulls off, without minding what Grandpapa said.

R is the Rose-bud, so cherish'd by all,
The pride of the cottage, the joy of the hall.

S is the Snow-drop, so drooping and pale,
Which heeds not the snow-storm, but bends to the gale.

T is the Tulip, which Eleanor fair,
Loving scarlet and orange, has placed in her hair.

V stands for Violets, prized in the Spring,
When the birds of the grove are first heard to sing.

W Water-lilies, whereon Fairies delight,
To dance in the Summer, when shines the moon bright.

X for Exotics, which Grandmamma sends,
That Fanny may garnish the room for her friends.

Y Yellow-lily, which John, with a crook,
Is trying to reach from the bank of the brook.

Z is for Zinnia, which has carried away
The prize at the Grand Show of Flowers to-day.

A stands for Ass, a hard-working beast,
Who loves on a diet of thistles to feast.

B for the Bees that fly out here and there,
And bring to the hives the sweet honey with care.

C for the Cows, in the shade of the trees;
They are chewing the cud, and seem quite at their ease.

D for Ducks, swimming, and playing together;
They care not for rain nor the stormiest weather.

FARMYARD ALPHABET

E for the Eggs, which we find in the nest;
They still feel quite warm, from the hen's downy breast.

F are the Fowls: the hens and the cocks.
Take care, my fine birdies, beware of the fox.

G is the Goat, with two kids young and gay;
They run to their mother, then scamper away.

H is the Horse, so sleek and so strong;
He draws the hay-cart to the meadow along.

I is the Island, where Johnny doth wish
To sit on the bank, in the summer, and fish.

K are the Kittens, that live in the stable;
They will catch all the mice as soon as they're able.

L is for Lucy, who waits at the stile,
And puts down the pail, for she's resting awhile.

M is the Milk, which is good, Pussy thinks,
And so, uninvited and slyly, she drinks.

N stands for the Nuts; and when lessons are done,
Two boys can go nutting much better than one.

O for the Owl, that prowling at night,
Steals chicks from our barn in the quiet moonlight.

P for some Pigs, which have strayed from their sty,
But of course will return there to bed by and by.

Q stands for the Quince I have plucked from a tree,
To flavor the tart Mary's making for me.

LEIGHTON, BROTHERS.

R for the Rabbits, white, spotted, and gray;
Just see how that little one nibbles away.

S for the Sheep, with their coats of soft wool;
They stand in the meadows so pleasant and cool.

T for the Turkey, who stately doth sail,
With long sweeping wings and wide-spreading tail.

V for the Vine, growing high on the wall;
Take care, little boy, or you surely will fall.

W's the Wagon: we've been working all day.
The horses are now going home for their hay.

X, on the barrel, shows the strength of the beer.
Lower it gently, it will bring us good cheer.

Y stands for our Farm-yard, where chicks love to feed
On the oats, and the barley, and other good seed.

Z is for Zachary, shutting the gate;
So Good Night, little children; it's getting quite late.

A's Arable land, for ploughing and sowing:
Wheat, barley, and oats upon it are growing.

B stands for the Barn where we all our crops store;
The chickens pick up the fallen grains at the door.

C stands for our Cows, which give plenty of milk;
The coat of dear Colly is softer than silk.

D stands for the Dairy, where butter we make,
And very great care of our cheeses we take.

JOHN BULL'S FARM ALPHABET

E stands for Eggs, which the poultry-girl finds;
The geese in the meadow this little lass minds.

F stands for Fowls, of which every kind,
From Cochin to Bantam, you'll at our farm find.

G stands for Geese—just see how they run!
To bite that poor woman they think will be fun.

H stands for Hay, which we all like to make;
Even dear little Norman a hayfork will take.

I stands for Ice, which the ploughman must break,
That he for the horses some water may take.

J's for John Bull, who this pretty farm owns;
He's watching the women who pick up the stones.

K's the Knife-cutter which chops up so neat,
The straw that in winter the cattle must eat.

L's for the Lambs, which so merrily bound,
When spring-time is come, o'er the daisy-starred ground.

M's for the Milkmaid—a pretty young lass,
Tripping with pail and stool over the grass.

N stands for the Nag, that trots on so well,
When John Bull goes to the market to sell.

O stands for Oats, which to horses we give;
The carter is bringing them, here, in a sieve.

P's for the Plough, which must win us our bread.
By means of the plough all the nations are fed.

Q stands for Quinces; a nice jam they make.
Mary would like a fine ripe one to take.

R stands for Reapers, who cut down the wheat:
When harvest is over they all have a treat.

S is the Sow, with her litter of pigs:
See how she's grunting, and in the earth digs.

T stands for Turkeys; a fat one there'll be
When Christmas comes for my brothers and me.

U is for Useful things, such as the drill,
The harrow, the pitchfork, and what else you will.
V is the Vine which grows on the house wall;
The grapes are quite sweet, and not very small.

W's the Waggon which bears the wheat home,
For now near the end of the harvest we're come.

X is for Xcellent,— such is our mother,
Our father, our sisters, and dear little brother.

Y is the Youth who the bird scares away;
When his work's over he runs off to play.

Z's for what Yorkshiremen call our "zmall things,"
Which, at last, to its ending our Alphabet brings.

WALTER CRANE'S
ABSURD A.B.C.

GEORGE ROUTLEDGE & SONS. Limited

A for the APPLE or Alphabet pie, Which all get a slice of. Come taste it & try.

C for the CAT that played on the fiddle, When cows jumped higher than 'Heigh Diddle, Diddle!'

D for the DAME with her pig at the stile, 'Tis said they got over, but not yet a while.

B is the BABY who gave Mr Bunting Full many a long days' rabbit skin hunting.

E for the Englishman,
ready to make fast
The giant who wanted to
have him for breakfast.

F for the Frog in the story,
you know,
Begun with a wooing but
ending in woe.

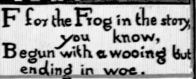

G for Goosey Gander
who wandered upstairs,
And met the old man
who objected to prayers.

H for poor Humpty who
after his fall.
Felt obliged to resign his
seat on the wall.

I for the Inn where they
wouldn't give beer,
To one with too much
and no money, I fear.

J does for poor Jack and
also for Jill,
Who had so disastrous
a tumble down hill.

K L M

L for Little man, gun and
bullets complete,
Who shot the poor duck, and
was proud of the feat.

K for calm Kitty, at dinner
who sat,
While all the good folks
watched the dog & the cat.

rous children
who
much for
er in Shoe

O the Old person that
cobwebs did spy,
And went up to sweep e'm
Oh ever so high!

M for Miss Muffet, with
that horrid spider,
ust dropped into tea and
a chat beside her.

P for the Pie made of
blackbirds to sing,
A song fit for supper
a dish for a king.

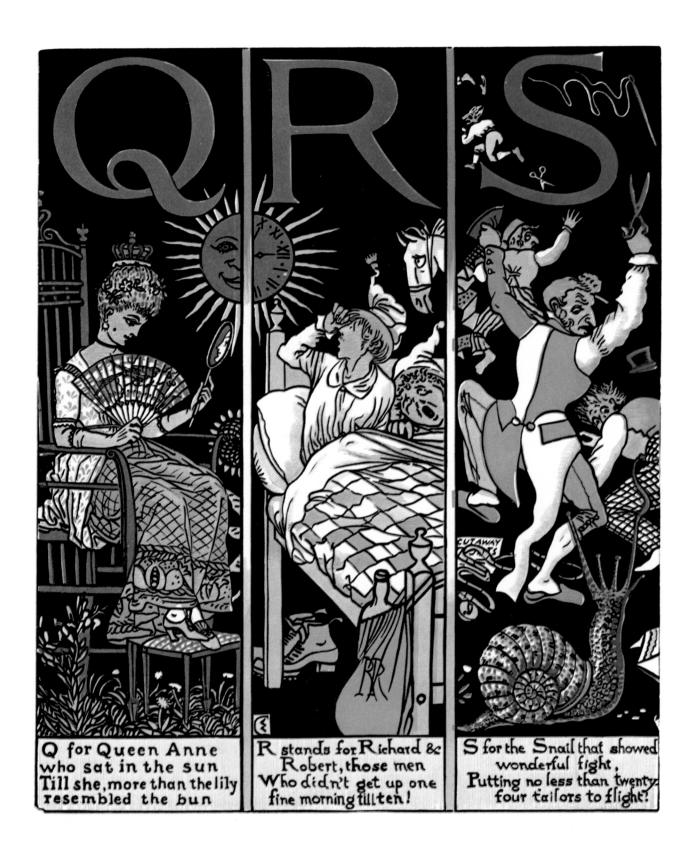

Q for Queen Anne
who sat in the sun
Till she, more than the lily
resembled the bun

R stands for Richard &
Robert, those men
Who didn't get up one
fine morning till ten!

S for the Snail that showed
wonderful fight,
Putting no less than twenty-
four tailors to flight!

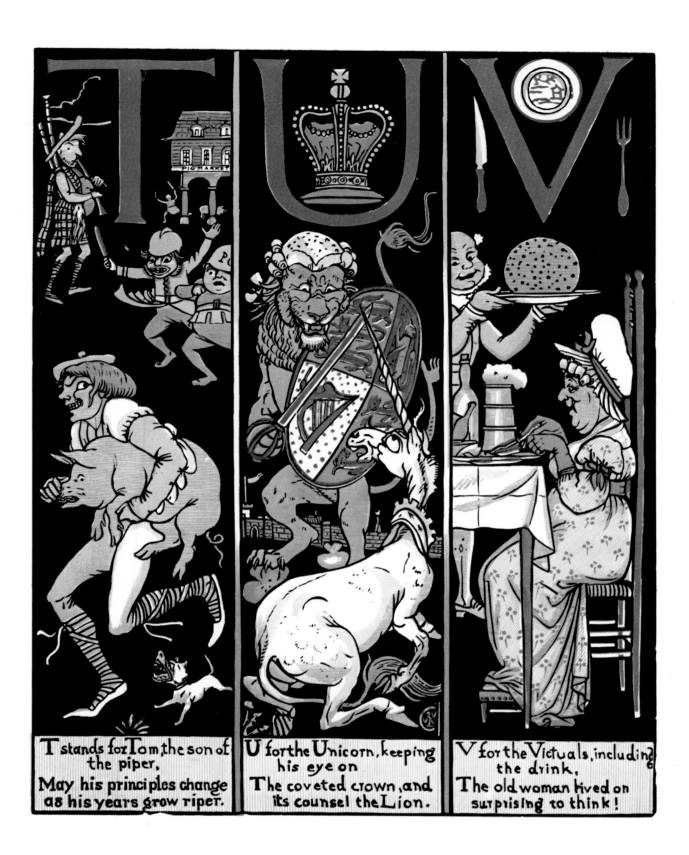

T stands for Tom, the son of
the piper,
May his principles change
as his years grow riper.

U for the Unicorn, keeping
his eye on
The coveted crown, and
its counsel the Lion.

V for the Victuals, including
the drink,
The old woman lived on
surprising to think!

W for the WOMAN who not over nice, Made very short work of the three blind mice

X is the X that is found upon buns, Which daughters not liking may come in for sons.

Y for Yankee Doodle of ancient renown, Both he & his pony that took him to town.

Z for the Zany who looked like a fool, For when he was young he neglected his school.

School Board

H h Hare Horse Hyena

I i Ibex

J j Jackal

K k
Kangaroo
Kid

L l
Leopard
Lizard

O
Otter
Ox

Monkey
Mouse

MNn
Noah

Pp
Pig
Porcupine

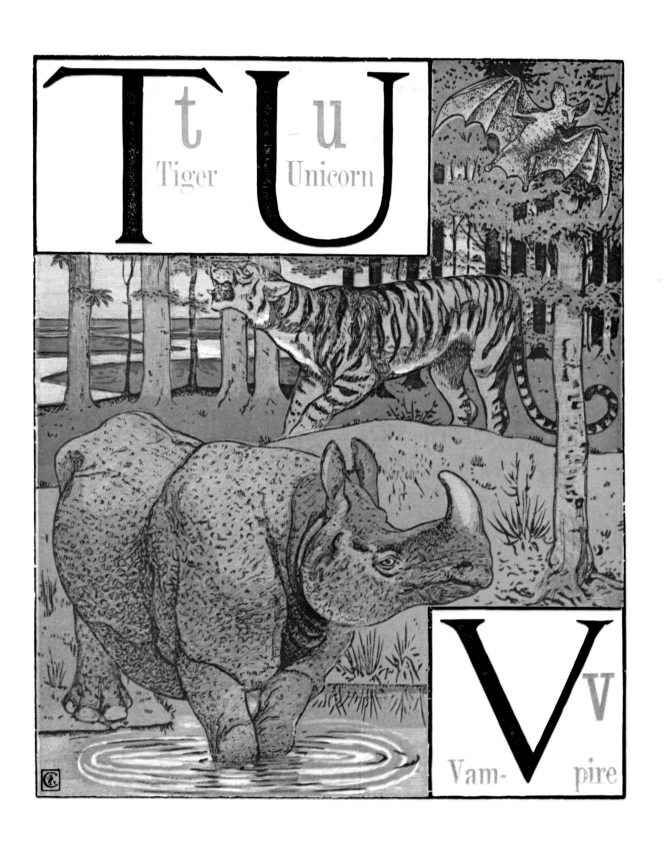

T t Tiger   U u Unicorn

V v Vam- pire

W X Y

W w Wolf

X x Xiphias

Y y Yak

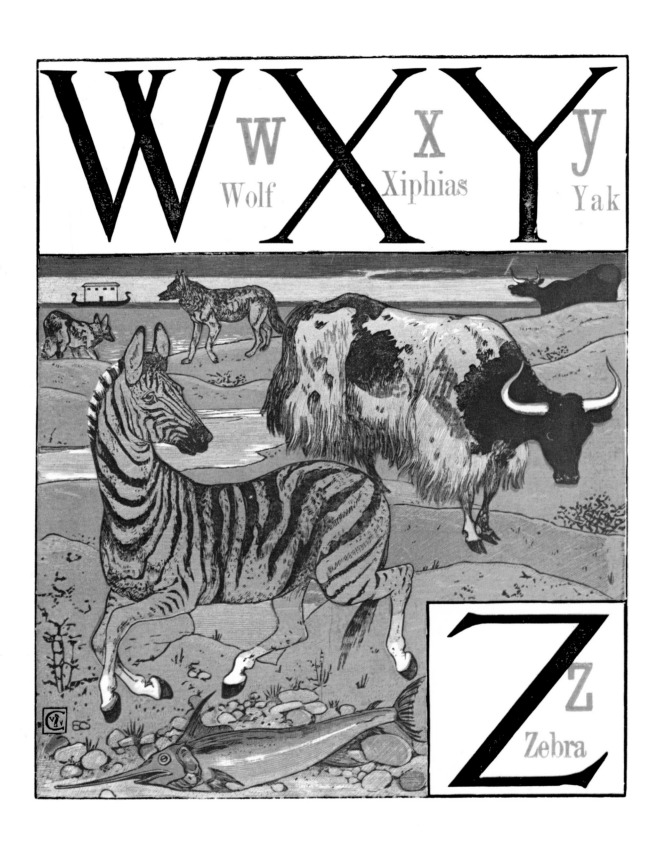

Z z Zebra

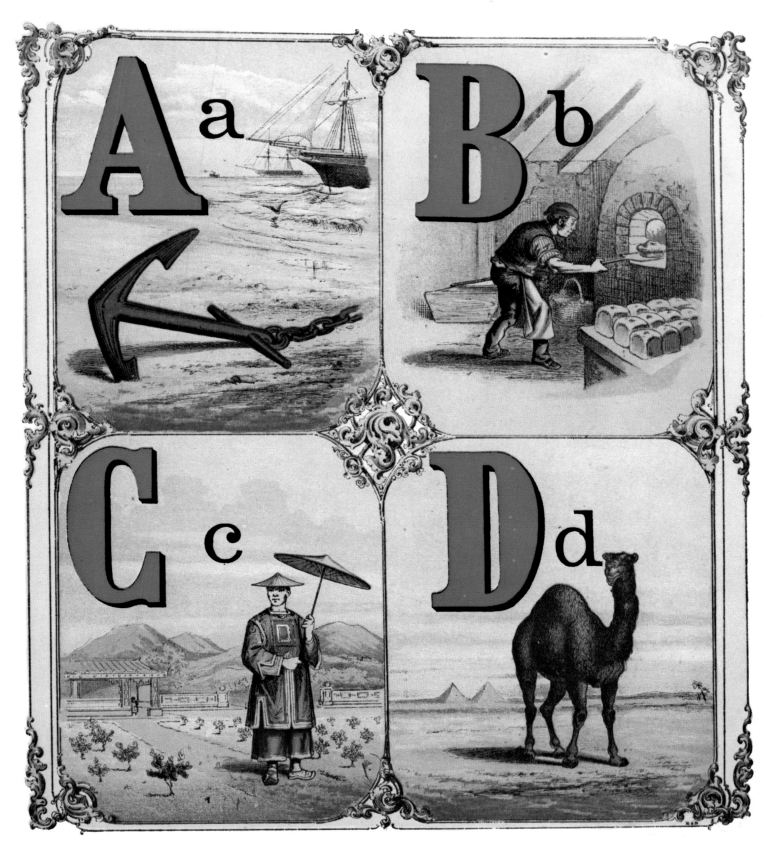

A stands for the Anchor we cast in the sea,
To hold the ship fast where we wish it to be.

B stands for the Baker who makes men their bread,
The great staff of life on which nations are fed.

C stands for a Chinaman; here one you see
Walking amidst his plantations of tea.

D for Dromedary; o'er deserts he strays,
And goes without water for many long days.

THE GLOBE ALPHABET

E stands for Elk, in cold countries he's found;
With Elks the American forests abound.

F stands for the Fruit that in summer we eat,
And find so refreshingly cooling and sweet.

G stands for Giraffe, which is able, you see,
To eat the top leaves from the branch of a tree.

H for Hippopotamus, savage and strong;
By African rivers he wanders along.

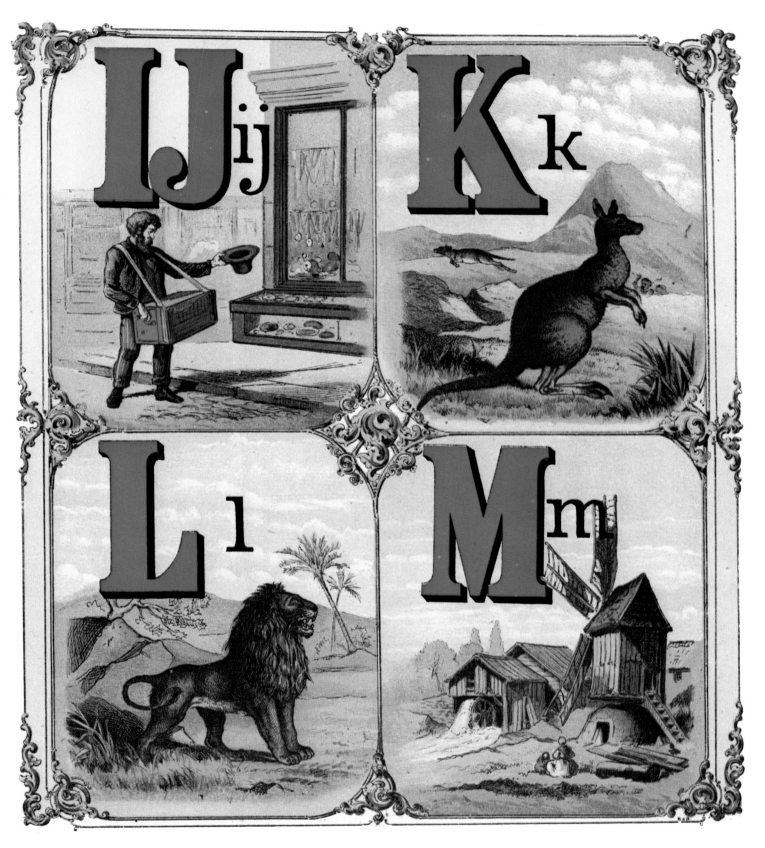

I's for Italian, an organ he grinds.
J is for Jewels of various kinds.

K stands for Kangaroos, sitting and leaping;
Hunters to kill them a keen watch are keeping.

L stands for the Lion, of forests the king;
With terrible roaring he makes the woods ring.

M stands for the Mill, where by water's great pow'r
The wheat is ground down to a very fine flour.

N stands for a Nabob, a lord of the East,
Who likes on strong coffee and sweetmeats to feast.

O stands for the Organ, delightful the sound
In church when its music floats solemnly round.

P stands for the Peacock, a bird very vain
Of feathers he sweeps on the earth like a train.

Q stands for Quadrille, which the little ones dance
As well, we all think, as the children in France.

R stands for Reindeer, very swiftly it goes
Carrying the Laplander over the snows.

S stands for the Sculptor, who statues can make,
And portraits with chisel and mallet can take.

T stands for the Tiger, a terrible beast,
That lives in the jungles and woods of the East.

U stands for the Uniform, in which are seen
The soldiers who fight for their country and Queen.

V stands for the Vulture, a great bird of prey.
W for the Waggon that carries the hay.

X for the Xylographer, cutting on wood
A picture, which printed he thinks will be good.

Y stands for the Yacht, that bounds o'er the sea:
A prettier cutter you don't often see.

Z stands for a Zebra, whose elegant shape
The sculptor, we think, for his model might take.

A stands for Anchor, Arrow, Antlers, Awl, Axe, Alphabet Book, Ark, Apples, A. B. C., Album.

B stands for Bell, Bottles, Beetroot, Barley, Bit, Bellows, Basin, Boat, Barrel, Broom, Boot, Bread, Basket, Ball, Bat.

C stands for Clock, Curtain, Cage, Cat, Cradle, Can, Candle, Chair, Cane.

D stands for Door, Dagger, Dish, Dumb-Bells, Dice, Decanter, Doll, Drum, Drumsticks, Dresser, Drawers, Dustpan.

E stands for Eye-Glass, Europe, Easel, Elephant, Egg Cup, Egg, Ewer, Envelope, Engine, England.

F stands for Fan, Feather, Fire-Place, Frying-Pan, Fish, Fender, Fork, Flask, File, Flag, Form, Funnel, Flower-Pot.

G stands for Goat, Globe, Gas Jet, Gun, Goblet, Grater, Glue Pot, Glove, Gimlet, Grammar.

H stands for Hat, Horn, Horseshoe, Hammer, Ham, Handle, Hoop, Harp, Hour Glass, Hamper, Hobby Horse, Hook.

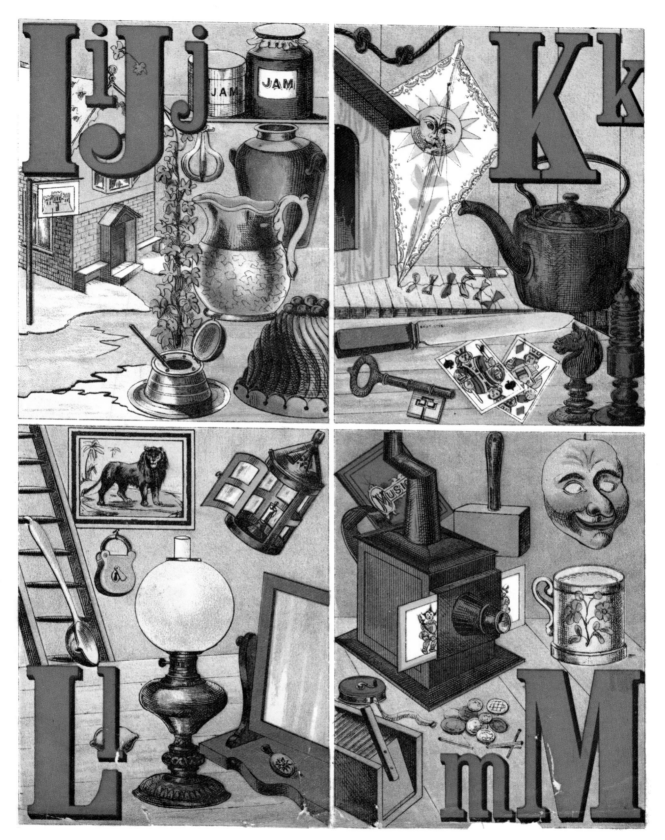

I stands for Inn, Ivy, Ice, Ink-Pot.

J stands for Jam, Jew's-Harp, Jar, Jug, Jelly.

K stands for Kennel, Knot, Kite, Kettle, Knife, Key, Kings, (Cards), Knight (Chess), King (Chess).

L stands for Ladder, Lion, Lamp, Ladle, Lock, Lantern, Lemon, Looking-Glass, Locket.

M stands for Music Book, Mallet, Mask, Measure, Magic Lantern, Mug, Mouse Trap, Money, Matches.

N stands for Needle, Necklace, Net, Night Light, Nine Pins, Nibs, Nail, Nest, Nuts, Nutcrackers.

O stands for Oar, Onions, Oven, Opera Glass, Oysters, Oranges, Oats.

P stands for Pepper, Palette, Plates, Pill Box, Pie, Pincushion, Pudding, Pencil, Pipe, Poker, Pail, Pitcher.

Q stands for Queen, Quiver, Quart, Quoits, Quill, Quires.

R stands for Rope, Rings, Rake, Reel, Rug, Rocking Horse, Rule, Rose, Rattle.

S stands for Sea Gulls, Sun, Sea, Ship, Steamer, Sand, Shell, Saw, Spade, Scissors, Slate, Spectacles.

T stands for Trumpet, Tub, Teapot, Tray, Tumbler, Table, Table Cloth, Tongs, Top, Thimble.

U stands for Unicorn, Union Jack, Urn, Umbrella.

V stands for Venetian Blind, Vase, Van, Violin, Violets.

W stands for Wind Mill, Well, Wine Glass, Watering Can, Wheelbarrow, Walking Stick, Whip, Whistle, Watch, Watch Key, Windlass.

X stands for Xmas Tree.

Y stands for Yacht, Yule Log.
Z stands for Zig-zag, Zebra, Zodiac.